Live Life with a Heart
Deeply Connected to God

Live Life with a Heart Deeply Connected to God:
"The Condition of Our Heart"

Pastor Wilbert L. Watson

Live Life with a Heart Deeply Connected to God

FOREWORD

JOHN 15:9-11, "AS THE FATHER LOVED ME, I ALSO HAVE LOVED YOU; ABIDE IN MY LOVE. IF YOU KEEP MY COMMANDMENTS, YOU WILL ABIDE IN MY LOVE, JUST AS I HAVE KEPT MY FATHER'S COMMANDMENTS AND ABIDE IN HIS LOVE. THESE THINGS I HAVE SPOKEN TO YOU, THAT MY JOY MAY REMAIN IN YOU, AND THAT YOUR JOY MAY BE FULL."

I wrote this book to inspire others to make a bold change to live a life with a heart that's deeply connected to God. It's important that our lifestyle pleases God instead of striving to impress people in the spiritual realm. I remember times when I felt changing my lifestyle was simply not given much thought. I thought I was exactly who I was born to be until I experienced so many missed opportunities, terrible decision-making and numerous disappointments in my life. The best decision I could ever have made in life is surrendering my heart totally to God and giving up worldly desires, awful lifestyle habits, some people in my life, and my inner circle; even people who were allegedly closer to me than others.

It was not easy to give up my old worldly lifestyle habits but sincerely surrendering to God helped me become a new creature in Christ Jesus. My decision to surrender my heart to God changed my mind and produced a lifestyle that ultimately changed my character. When I decided to make a bold change in my life; this resulted in losing so-called friends and even some family members who I truly loved dearly from the bottom of my heart.

I meet people virtually every day who needed and wanted to change their lifestyles but refuse to make a bold commitment to change. Some believed they cannot change their corrupted habits, lifestyles and God will not forgive them.

The breakdown is mostly self-discipline and loss of self-control; they are sold-out to the worldly things and individual worldly desires and fleshly pleasures. If you sincerely desire a heart that is deeply connected to God and a lifestyle that pleases Him, this book is to encourage you to start today.

I must honestly express that changing from a worldly attitude to a godly attitude was not easy for me either. Our old pleasurable and pleasing worldly desires feel good but when you make a truthful determination to serve God wholeheartedly, you can be in charge of your habits and thinking with the guidance of the Holy Spirit. I was determined not to give up but boldly stepped out, and let God transform my life to a standard of living that's pleasing to Him. Romans 7:15 is an awesome scripture to read and meditate on: In this scripture, Paul shares his struggle like ours today. He said, *"I don't understand what I am doing. For I don't do what I want to do, but instead do what I hate."* In true believers, the Holy Spirit dwells within them and will guide them in the spiritual warfare between the flesh and the Spirit. You too can make a decision to serve God wholeheartedly even through facing temptation head on.

Psalm 12:6 says, "And the words of the Lord are flawless, like silver purified in a crucible, gold refined seven times." God's Word is important for us to stay connected to His heart.

Live Life with a Heart Deeply Connected to God

I encourage you to read God's Word (the Bible) because it reveals the truth about ourselves, others and shows us pure godly knowledge and wisdom. God's Word helps me daily to maintain a deep spiritual connection with Him. After becoming a preacher of the gospel in 2005, I learned so much more about God's love and how to even go deeper in my relationship with Him. I encourage others to cultivate and achieve a deeper relationship with God by making Him the first priority in their lives and through prayer and reading His Word.

Table of Contents

CHAPTER 1

IN THE HEART

The word heart is used over 900 times in the Bible (the Word of God); I express this point because it reflects how important the heart truly is to God. Jeremiah 17:9-11(NIV) reads, [9]The heart is deceitful above all things and beyond cure. Who can understand it? [10]"I the LORD search the heart and examine the mind, to reward each person according to their conduct, according to what their deeds deserve." [11]Like a partridge that hatches eggs it did not lay are those who gain riches by unjust means. When their lives are half gone, their riches will desert them, and in the end, they will prove to be fools.

If the ways of blessing and cursing are so clear in God's Word, why would anyone choose the path of sin? I realize after reading, praying and meditating on Jeremiah 17:9-11, the cause for such conflict or fighting in the heart is it deceitfulness. I did not understand for a while that the heart could be so deceitful and kind of ponder on Jeremiah's meaning "wondered who could even understand it."

Live Life with a Heart Deeply Connected to God

God answered Jeremiah by letting him know that He can search the heart and examine the mind. God knows our deepest thoughts, secrets and motives that we as individuals might hide from others. Consequently, God could justly render or give each person what he or she truly deserves. The principle of judgment was applied to those who had amassed or cumulated riches by using unjust or undeserved means: If a partridge hatched the eggs of another bird, the offspring (the young) would soon desert (leave) from the mother and fly away. So, wealth that had been acquired unjustly would be taken away, and the one who had been hoarding it would be exposed as a fool. Jeremiah's solution to sin was to focus on the majesty or splendor of God.

This chapter is titled "In the Heart." However, I am not speaking about the physical heart; I am speaking about the divine nature spiritual heart that God wants His true believers to possess. The heart is the very center of our spiritual being similar to the organ of our physical body. As the heart (physical) is the key to life and death, in the Word of God, the heart is the very center of our life.

In Acts 8:21, Peter said to Simon, the sorcerer, *"For thy heart is not right in the sight of God."*

Peter is not speaking about a diseased heart; he is speaking about the fact that Simon did not have his life totally surrendered to God. His affections, his motives, his desires were not according to the will of God. The heart is the center, of our personality: With the heart, man thinks (Hebrews 4:12); With the heart, man reasons (Mark 2:6-8); With the heart, man understands (Matthews 13:15); With the heart, man believes (Romans 10:9, 10); The heart has emotions (Matthews 22: 36-29), and the heart wills, purposes, or determines!

God wants us all to have a new spiritual heart that is aligned with His will and purpose for our lives. God wants us to have a spiritual heart transformation by being born again because the old sinful heart is incurably or terminally wicked and hopeless. But God alone can perform the miracle of a complete transformation of the heart. We cannot fix our spiritual heart alone or patch it up; we need God. He alone can give us a new heart.

I encourage you to sincerely understand that God truly does know our heart and secrets. Psalm 139:23-24 says, "God looks on the heart; He knows what is in your heart." In reading Chapter 1 of this book, you may be asking or thinking, "do I need a new heart?"

Let me help you, we all need a new heart. Why? Because God heals. He is the great physician and He can heal anyone who wants to be heal from any afflictions. I am a "keeping it real" kind of person; there are going to be times in our lives when we will need God to heal us or a loved one. If you truly desire in your heart to have a new heart; I encourage you not to be ashamed or afraid. I ask that you pray to God for a new spiritual heart that is pleasing to Him.

When you make that eternal decision to serve God wholeheartedly and faithfully; your mind and heart are opened to positive healings, and amazing things start happening to you. If we love God with all of our heart, it will be evident through Jesus Christ. Psalm 91:14, says, "Because he loves me," says the LORD, "I will rescue him; I will protect him, for he acknowledges my name. We must spend time with God to have a heart like his heart. Spiritual life begins in the heart, and it begins with God. God also has a heart (Acts 13:22) and has emotions and desires which drive His behavior toward His creatures.

The Lord desires that all people be saved and come to the knowledge of the truth" (1 Timothy 2:4). So, to have a deeply connected heart and an intimate personal relationship with God; one must have no excuses.

Be completely open and honest with God; surrender to God totally with an open and honest heart.

It's important to understand that joy comes from the heart not necessarily from our outward circumstances or situation. Life can present some really challenging seasons or bring difficulties that are very troubling at times. I am so glad that God sees these things that can cause major issues in our heart and mind if not careful. God works deeply into our inner thoughts and desires, but He primarily looks at our heart. This way He can show us from the inside what and why we do certain things (right or wrong). God is with us and His own heart is for His people; God sees and knows the heart of all people.

It has to be in your heart to want to serve the Lord; even through trials and tribulations. If it is in your heart to serve the Lord wholeheartedly; you will be eager to be used by God for His glory. I am in no way saying that I am perfect but I know with all diligence in serving God, godly wisdom can be obtained and demonstrated from the heart. *Matthew 20:26 reads, "Not so with you. Instead, whoever wants to become great among you must be your servant."* This scripture proves that God is interested in a servant's heart, attitude, and how he or she treats others.

A nasty attitude reveals a lot about a person's character and attitude. So, if one has it in his or her heart to serve the Lord wholeheartedly, they can serve God like a servant should and love their brothers and sisters in Christ Jesus. When it's in your heart to serve the Lord, its's important to reflect the nature of God to everyone.

Over the past 25 years, loving God with all my heart has become so strong and sincere. I made time for God each day to continue an intimate relationship, no matter who favors me or not. I communicated to God through prayer and conversation. I found myself on numerous occasions thinking with a divided mind but God helped me change that with His love. Once I knew more about God and His Word and sincerely put Him first my life, my thinking and behavior became properly aligned with God.

Make God your first priority and see how you and your life change. God is manifested by loving us but we must make sure our love is for Him and not the things in this confusing world. Love God with all of your heart, soul, mind, and strength; by doing this, the worldly things in this world will become less distracting. If we are not careful, worldly distractions can keep us from salvation.

I don't know about you, but I want to live according to God's truth, not the world. Stay in God's word and keep 1 Corinthians 10:13 close by when temptation comes: *"No temptation has overtaken you that is not common to man. God is faithful, and he will not let you be tempted beyond your ability, but with the temptation he will also provide the way of escape, that you may be able to endure it."*

Notes:

_____

_____

_____

_____

_____

_____

_____

_____

_____

_____

_____

_____

_____

_____

CHAPTER 2

BEING HOLY IS AN ATTITUDE OF THE HEART

Being holy is an attitude of the heart; 1 Thessalonians 5:22(NIV) reads, "reject every kind of evil." We need to know certainly without a doubt that Biblical holiness is the state of the heart, in devotion to God which controls the believer's life and directs him or her to "abstain from even the appearance of evil." One does not become holy by looking a certain way or dressing up his or her outward appearance or even actions! A great example of a person who is holy, walks around all day, smiling, making religious statements, glowing with a halo above his or her head, and absolutely unlike you or me. We all strive to live clean godly lives, which is a sign of holiness, but genuine Christians know they are no better than anyone else.

The bumper sticker we often see on cars reads: "Christians are not perfect, they are just forgiven." Some denominations and Christian sects wear different clothes, no make-up, comb their hair in a particular way, and generally try to look plain and think that makes the look holy than others. I am sure you probably have experienced, heard or seen; even some churches where they promote "standards" such as dress codes and rules to live by for their members and those who come to Church. Please don't misunderstand my expression; I honestly don't have any problem with godly standards, but often they are taken to the extreme and are substituted for genuine Christian living.

For example, have you ever visited a church and seen at the entrance of the front door with a sign saying, "No long hair or women in pants?" So, if a lost man with long hair came to their church, he would not be welcome, or women who came wearing women's pants. Now, trust me; something is definitely wrong with that kind of thinking by so-called Christians. This kind of thinking has deterred or discouraged many people from attending any Church, especially the younger generation. This kind of thinking and practice are nonsense and is the same philosophy of the Pharisees. Some sincere churches truly misunderstand what the Lord meant when he told Christians not be conformed to the world in Romans 12:2. Let me emphasize my point: wearing black clothes or a particular dress, having a certain religious or "holier than thou" appearance does not make one holy.

Live Life with a Heart Deeply Connected to God

I almost certain that I am not the only one who have heard people say, "I am not Holier than Thou!" I believe I can assist you in the origin of "I am not Holier than Thou!" This saying is believed to have come from Isaiah 65:5 (KJV), "come not near me, for I am holier than thou!" My beloved brothers and sisters in Christ Jesus, if someone is "Holier-than-thou!" they are Holier than God. Conversely, it also literally means holier than me or better than me. When a person has taken the moral high ground or just up themselves; they are being "Holier-than-thou!" Just because one made one foolish mistake; does not mean you and anybody else gets to give him or her "holier-than-thou attitude!"

People who are "holier-than-thou" think that they are morally honourably better than anyone else. "Holier than thou" is a phrase used to describe someone who acts superior to others or is perceived to act that way! Typically, the phrase refers to an attitude that places an individual above others on a moralistic or high-minded level. Although no one is perfect, this outlook might lead a person to be quick to point out other people's flaws but rarely notice his or her own flaws. The term or phrase often refers to someone so pious (religious or self-righteous) and devoted in his or her beliefs that he or she judges others, which many people consider to be exactly the opposite of the biblical warning "judge not lest ye be judged." The word "thou" originates from Old English. Although it is used as an ordinary pronoun meaning "you," it was once used in certain Bible translations to refer exclusively to God and was capitalized. When considered in light of this knowledge, the phrase "holier than thou" might be interpreted to mean putting oneself above God.

The attitude of the biblical Pharisees, a group of religious leaders who were very devout in their beliefs might be interpreted as "holier than thou." According to the books of the New Testament, the Pharisees adhered so strictly to religious laws that they opposed Jesus doing good works on the Sabbath. In so doing, their attitude was said to have been a transgression of the law because in their self-righteousness, they placed themselves above God.

Generally, the idea of being holy has been misunderstood by most people (both past and present). Jesus reprimanded the teachers of the Law and the Pharisees for not understanding the true meaning of being holy (Matthew 6: 23). Being holy is not about showing people how righteous we are: telling them how much we give to the poor, showing them how much we are doing for the Church, or telling them how often we fast and do

Live Life with a Heart Deeply Connected to God

penance (Matthew 6:1-18). It is also not about what we wear, where we sit and how people address us (Matthew 23:5-1).

The parable of the Good Samaritan teaches us that holiness has nothing to do with a person's race, nationality or career or profession as the Samaritan could love his neighbor more than the priest and Levite (Luke 10:29-37). Holiness is "the state of the heart," in devotion to God which controls the believer's life and directs him to "avoid evil, wherever it may be." We need to know without confusion and the negative influence of others what it means to be holy! Being Holy is an attitude of the heart. A person who in his heart does not see himself or herself as totally dedicated to the Lord's service could dress right, look right, talk right and act right, but still not be living a holy life. The Lord does not look at the things people look at. People look at the outward appearance, but the LORD looks at the heart." (1 Samuel 16:7) I read an article titled: Holiness: "The Heart God Purifies," by Nancy Demoss Wolgemuth (2020). She implies, "to most believers, holiness is a concept that evokes mixed emotions and at best, seems shrouded in mystery. But no word better captures the splendor of who God is and the destination to which He has called us. The call to pursue holiness is an invitation to experience the blessings and joys of intimacy with God, to be free from the weight and the burden of sin, and to become all He created us to be." I completely agree with Wolgemuth's article because I actually see this type of attitude or concept mentality displayed by many professed Christians nowadays.

If a person's heart has not been developed like God's heart; it is very difficult for that person to reflect holiness from their heart. I strived to instill in my children and others how to have a heart that is holy and respond to the gospel of Jesus Christ. I always start with showing them how to be humble with a teachable spirit and understanding that pride will hinder their trust in God, and a heart for God. Also, pray because prayer is the most effective weapon we have and the source of power we need to communicate with God. We can pray to God to restrain or remove things that are no like Him from our heart. Remove all unholiness that may try to come against us, especially during our seasons of weakness. God desires to hear from us; He wants us to hear us say what's on our hearts and minds.

A heart that is holy reflects an attitude of wholeheartedness and dedication to serving God. This verse shows when one's heart contains the Holy Spirit and the presence of the Lord reigns.

Live Life with a Heart Deeply Connected to God

God loves us and we can always count on His love in our hearts when we truly seek him first.

Notes:_____

_____

_____

_____

_____

_____

_____

_____

_____

_____

_____

_____

_____

_____

_____

_____

_____

_____

CHAPTER 3

FULLY COMMITTED HEART

This chapter is near and dear to my heart because trying to serve God with an uncommitted or "casual" heart is eternally perilous to our soul. Serving as a Pastor for over 16 years has revealed many people who have good intentions within their hearts to work hard but their heart (spiritual) is not fully committed to God. Their hearts are entirely committed to pleasing people for their praise. Lip service does not please God but whole-heartedness does please God.

2 Chronicles 16:10, reads "For the eyes of the LORD range throughout the earth to strengthen those whose hearts are fully committed to him." If you have not taken the first step toward commitment to God, today can be the day. Think about what's keeping you from having a fully committed heart to God. Could it be worldly and fleshly desires? Perhaps you are holding back a part of yourself! A fully committed heart to God means welcoming God wherever you go and thanking Him for blessing you each day.

Live Life with a Heart Deeply Connected to God

When you are fully committed to God, your spiritual senses are increased. You will start seeing miracles in your life and actually hear when God speaks to you.

God is looking for people whose hearts are fully committed to Him. Being a genuine Christian involves a sincere commitment that's not part-time but serving God in every part of our lives. A heart that is devoted to God is totally surrendered and allows one to love and worship God in Spirit and in Truth. He is an awesome God and is in our lives. When we made or make the decision to follow Jesus Christ, we must follow Jesus' ways, not ours. Jesus wants us to do far more than simply agree with Him or even believe in Him; He wants us to give our entire lives over to Him and follow after Him with total commitment. God wants us to love Him with all of our heart; He wants more than obedience. Not only does He want us to obey the letter of the law, He wants us to agree with the spirit of the law in our hearts!

I realized many years ago I had a desire and a heart to serve God wholeheartedly but allowed myself to become vulnerable to Satan's attacks and tricks. I let myself, family and others down; a few times, I acted so irresponsibly because of the onset of anger, foolish thoughts and mistakes.

I was momentarily in the dump and made some irresponsible choices that I would normally not do or allow in my life that came in like a flood. But one day I when woke up! I repented and promised God that I would serve Him. No matter the outcomes on my decision to serve Him wholeheartedly; fear of anyone, anybody or anything won't stop me. I said, Lord, I am all yours! I surrender my whole heart to You. After that day, I must be honest; I suffered and endured some difficult times, pains, disappointments and regrets of hurting others and myself because of my irresponsible actions and conduct. I felt so worthless to God, myself and others. I did not like those worthless feelings, so I prayed and ask God to purge me and filled me up with His will and desires for my life.

I encourage you to make sure your heart is fully committed to God before it's too late. I mentioned earlier in this chapter that I repented and ask God to fill me up with His will and desires for my life. I knew repentance was good for me in order to maintain a personal relationship with God. Repentance means to turn from that which is unholy towards that which is holy. It means to turn away from sin and move towards God. Repentance begins when we realize that our hearts are not in accordance with God and we willingly submit our wills to God's will as it is

Live Life with a Heart Deeply Connected to God

revealed in the Bible. We discover our need to do this when we compare ourselves to the Lord Jesus. We discover this when we compare ourselves to the word of God. After repentance comes commitment! Commitment to God and His word should be the heart of every Christian.

After all, Jesus said, "those whom He knows hear His voice and follow Him (John 10:27-28)." That is, they follow what Jesus says and do what He does.

I ask that you honestly see the kind of a Christian that you are?

God is not where our sin is, God is not where rebellion to His Word is. God is not in the world that seeks to use the Church as a social instrument, nor with the Christian who wants to change the church and make it more "tolerant (or liberal)," God is not in the hearts of the cold who do not take His words seriously, but instead give casual regard to it only when it agrees with their feelings and wants. I hear and see people who give a lot of lip service but God knows all things, including what is in our heart! God knows what's in our heart and thoughts! Actions done with bad motives are despised by God! Our level of commitment to God really matters; determine within your own heart who you will serve.

Live Life with a Heart Deeply Connected to God

The COVID-19 pandemic revealed a lot of people's true colors (true character); many who were supposedly faithful and fully committed to God commitment fell like they were never born again. Members in the churches worldwide turned their back on God and His new covenant. This pandemic exposed numerous professed "born again" Christians' true character but also their true level of unfaithfulness and upsetting or disappointing level of commitment they in God. It's important that our level of commitment to God truly display that God is a priority in our lives. God always have our back in any situation or circumstance. His commitment to us and His promises are amazingly merciful and graceful!

Notes:

_____

_____

_____

_____

_____

_____

_____

CHAPTER 4

A HEART PROBLEM

Have you ever met someone who was just plain stubborn as a mule or mulish? You might know some people within your own circle of friends or family who insist on having their way. If it's not their way, it's the highway. I have plenty of experiences because I am sometimes surrounded by plenty who are just plain stubborn, hardheaded and with critical spirits; they are very determined and uncompromising. They are most times uncompromising and set in their ways. If they don't hear or get what they want, they are gone and don't want to have anything to with you or me. God says these people have a hardened heart. These harden heart or heart problem has existed since the beginning of time.

You may recall or remember Pharaoh in the Bible; he had a serious heart problem. He was presented with tremendous or overwhelming evidence; plague after plague, sign after sign and miracle after miracle, but still, Pharaoh refused to accept God's warnings and let the Israelites go.

Does this sound like anybody you know? God repeatedly presented Pharaoh with the truth of who He was, yet, Pharaoh would not bow. Even when faced with undeniable evidence that he was wrong, Pharaoh would not give in to God. Pharaoh refused to acknowledge that another Kingdom was greater than his. I am going somewhere with this, stay with me!

Hebrews 3:12-13 reads, "12 *Take heed, brethren, lest there be in any of you an evil heart of unbelief in departing from the living God. 13 But exhort one another daily while it is called Today; lest any of you be HARDENED THROUGH the deceitfulness of sin."*

Pharaoh's pride, stubbornness, and hard-heartedness caused him great grief and distress. His over-exposure and under response to truth proved to be extremely costly for him, his family, and his kingdom. All of us have experienced the stubborn desire to have things the way we want them, even when "our way" is not God's way. That's what Pharaoh was doing; if we are wise, we will learn from his experience. The Bible is very clear that a man, who is rebellious, is a man whose heart is not right (Psalm 78:8).

If I read this scripture to many Churches; folks will say they are being judged. Yes, they are by God not the messenger or reader of God's Word. We all need to honestly ask ourselves: *Is my heart right with God?* God wants us to know just where our heart is; is our heart in a relationship with God and Jesus Christ or is it in a relationship with the world in which we live? ***The "heart problem" of not being right with God is the original heart disease. It has been in existence since Adam first sinned in the Garden of Eden. As a matter of fact; even people we work with, live with or even fellowship within and out of the Church.***

A hardened heart problem is a major stronghold issue for many believers. *How does believer's heart become hardened? Hebrews 3:12-13 (NIV), says: "¹²See to it, brothers and sisters, that none of you has a sinful, unbelieving heart that turns away from the living God. ¹³But encourage one another daily, as long as it is called "Today," so that none of you may be hardened by sin's deceitfulness."*

Live Life with a Heart Deeply Connected to God

A believer's heart becomes hard heartened or hardened by refusing God's word, despising His work, and being ignorant or misinformed of his ways. We must understand as believers that sin is deceitful. There are many who think they are getting away with sin but all the while, it is hardening their hearts and robbing them of God's blessings. What makes it really bad; people with harden hearts know the truth. They know God's Word but constantly resist and refuse to obey it. They even know that God chastens or discipline disobedient and rebellious children, but they practically defy or dare God to act. They think they can sin and get away with it. I inform believers and nonbelievers not to ignore or neglect God's Word. I even back it up with

God's Hebrews 2:1-4 as the scripture or passage as a warning to believers to pay attention to what God says in His Word: "

[1]We must pay the most careful attention, therefore, to what we have heard, so that we do not drift away. [2]For since the message spoken through angels was binding, and every violation and disobedience received its just punishment,

³how shall we escape if we ignore so great a salvation? This salvation, which was first announced by the LORD, was confirmed to us by those who heard him. ⁴God also testified to it by signs, wonders and various miracles, and by gifts of the Holy Spirit distributed according to his will. "

Wife would say: we all want things the way WE want them. We all want what we want when we want it; I am more comfortable when things are the way I like them. Most people are naturally comfortable when things are going their way but the tension or problem comes into play when what we want is not what God wants. When the two conflict, refusal to act on the truth, time and time again will corrode the heart of man until nothing can melt (dissolve) the hardness. This chapter is to help you and many others avoid certain to show up into your path. Understand God's Word and warning against a hardened heart and the danger signs. If we don't heed or pay attention to the warning signs, we are   rationalizing ourselves into disaster. Rebellion is an open door to demonic spirits in a person's life. The Bible strictly warns against rebellion, and its consequences are not to be taken lightly. God's Word tells us that rebellion is in the same category of sin as witchcraft itself: *1 Samuel 15:23, "For rebellion is as the sin of witchcraft..."*

Rebellion cuts a person off from God; God's Word is clear that rebellion is a great way to find yourself in dry land spiritually! **The Bible says in Romans 3:23, *"for all have sinned and fall short of the glory of God."*** God also shows that rebellion shuts a person's ears from being able to hear God when He tries to speak to them (Ezekiel 12:2). Pharaoh's heart was hardened; he did not listen to the people as the people or as the Lord said. People with stubborn and rebellious hearts are in danger! They have turned away and departed from God. They refuse to listen to God's Word because they walk in the stubbornness of their hearts and have gone to other gods to serve them and bow down to them. God words say, *"let them be just like this waistband which is totally worthless."* If you believe you have a hardened and stubborn heart regarding the Lord and you fall in the category or group clearly specified in Romans 2:5: *"But because of your stubbornness and your unrepentant heart, you are storing up wrath against yourself for the day of God's wrath, when his righteous judgment will be revealed."*

Live Life with a Heart Deeply Connected to God

If this, is you, I encourage you to repent so you can open your heart and receive the Lord with a sincere heart and not speak with arrogance, pride or self-important. If your heart is hardening because of sin or rebellious; you need a new heart (meaning spiritually & mind). Forsake your rebellion, and turn to the Lord. Repent of your ways and receive God's mercy. Rebellion is an open door to demonic spirits in a person's life. God's Word warns us that rebellion darkens our spiritual eyesight (meaning our discernment), and it deafens our ears to hear God's voice! Having the right relationship with God begins with acknowledging your sin.

Next comes a humble confession of your sin to God! Preferring any earthly thing over God is a clear sign that our hearts have wandered (drift away). If you find yourself astray, discover how to get back in God's empowering grace. Get somewhere quiet and pray for God to soften your heart and help you feel His love. Just try to relax and open up to Him and let all your pain dissolve (just melt). A right heart is a new heart (Ezekiel. 36:26); ask God to create in you a clean heart and get rid of the heart problem.

CHAPTER 5

THE HEART MUST CHANGE

In praying, reading and meditating on Mark 7:15-23 of God's Word, I discovered a lot about why our heart must change to please God and to enter the kingdom of God. In Mark 7:15-23 (KJV),

> "[15] There is nothing outside a person that by going into him can defile him, but the things that come out of a person are what defile him."[16][a] [17] And when he had entered the house and left the people, his disciples asked him about the parable. [18] And he said to them, "Then are you also without understanding? Do you not see that whatever goes into a person from outside cannot defile him, [19] since it enters not his heart but his stomach, and is expelled?" [b] (Thus he declared all foods clean.) [20] And he said, "What comes out of a person is what defiles him. [21] For from within, out of the heart of man, come evil thoughts, sexual immorality, theft, murder, adultery,

[22] coveting, wickedness, deceit, sensuality, envy, slander, pride, foolishness. [23] All these evil things come from within, and they defile a person."

I learned that that the scribes and Pharisees became more vocal in their opposition to Jesus. The breach between true spirituality and man-made traditions drastically expanded. The teaching of man's law and traditions (referring to Elders, scribes and Pharisees) were not scripture-based. Jesus enters into an argument by calling His adversaries hypocrites. Like many today with the Pharisees mentality, many are not genuine Christians or true believers in Christ Jesus. I must emphasize that Jesus gives us the freedom of choice to be hypocrites or children of the most high God. According to God's Word, the Pharisees were not genuine Christians; they played a part for everyone to see. They were remarkable actors and played many characters. Jesus made a bold public statement that must have liberated His listeners and infuriated or made the Pharisees angry.

Live Life with a Heart Deeply Connected to God

Unless we are extremely careful, religious rituals can create serious problems. This is one of the reasons I stick to preaching and teaching God's Word. Man-made traditions can create a problem but some people will be miss entering heaven because of religious rituals.

In many churches, man-made rituals get more attention and authority than God's Word. They may be given as much authority as God's Word for many people because of their lack of knowledge and wisdom concerning God's Word. I encourage people under my leadership as a Pastor to pray, study, and meditate on God's Word. Stay focus on God and His Word; keep it in your heart because you will need it every day to go against Satan and his demonic angels. It's important to know the difference between God's will and man's empty traditions. I want to help as many people as I can to have a changed heart that's aligned with God's Word, not external religious man-made traditions or rituals.

God wants believers to have a purified heart that is only by faith. Scriptures show that defilement comes from within and not to blame others. We do have to look out for false prophets who profess to be true prophets but secretly or privately, they are like ferocious wolves.

But eventually, what's really on the inside of hypocrites will be revealed. Even though we worship with people who pretend they love and obey the Lord with all of their heart, mind and soul; they are not genuine; their fruit will eventually be recognized.

Matthew 5:8 reads, *"Blessed are the pure in heart: for they shall see God."* Perhaps you or other you may know is asking the Lord to "Create in me a clean heart." You are thinking, oh God renew a right spirit within me. If so, don't be afraid; come clean with God. Help others after you to establish a sincere relationship with God. The Lord will free us from falsehood with a divine personal relationship with Him. I know I had a lot of issues with my heart and became a new creature in Christ Jesus.

When I made the decision to serve God wholeheartedly, Satan started his attacks on me and I lost many so-called true friends. In some cases, family members too! God changed my heart and I refused to change back to my old lifestyle and old friends still placing worldly or material things before God. You too can have a clean heart today! You can become free from hidden motives, selfishness and lack of consideration for others.

Live Life with a Heart Deeply Connected to God

Our biggest problem is not external but internal; all of us have a heart problem. In order for a person to be saved, then the heart must be changed. This only happens by the power of God in response to faith. "With the heart one believes unto righteousness" (Romans 10:10).

Notes:

_____

_____

_____

_____

_____

_____

_____

_____

_____

_____

_____

_____

_____

_____

CHAPTER 6

IT'S WHAT WE DO WITH OUR HEART

The Word of God is very specific about how you as a Christian are to conduct yourself toward the non-Christian. Read Colossians 4:5-6 and you will see what **God** wants you, as a Christian to do. The literal translation of Colossians. 4:5-6 is in wisdom; walk toward the ones outside, redeeming the time.

Ephesians 4:17-19 "[17]*So I tell you this, and insist on it in the LORD, that you must no longer live as the Gentiles do, in the futility of their thinking.* [18]*They are darkened in their understanding and separated from the life of God because of the ignorance that is in them due to the hardening of their hearts.* [19]*Having lost all sensitivity, they have given themselves over to sensuality so as to indulge in every kind of impurity, and they are full of greed."*
On this day, if you are not yet a believer and you feel God tugging at your hard heart, then run toward God because you are worthy because God does not call everyone to Himself. You are being given an opportunity for eternal life which only God can grant.

When we give our hearts to God, we love with all we have. This means we focus our attention on Him and grow to desire His will for our lives. I know this may sound impossible but it is not. When we give our hearts to the Lord, He gives us the Holy Spirit, who comes to live in our hearts. If we allow the Holy Spirit to guide us, He will safeguard our hearts against self-destructive sin and inspire us to serve God and others. It's what we do with our hearts; for instance, the heart is a muscle at the center of the body; through contraction and relaxation, it sustains life. When it stops working, we cease to be alive. Yet a heart is more than an organ that pumps blood. Likewise, in relation to us as genuine believers in Christ Jesus; in the Bible, the heart is a metaphor or symbol for the most sensitive areas of our lives, the place from which our passions are aroused and our worst plans are conceived. Out of all the areas in life that force us to take "security measures," the Bible presents our effort to protect our heart as the most important of all. So, we must be diligent or careful to keep our hearts; because the condition of our heart will affect everything else in our life. It's what we do with our heart because our heart determines what we do with our life.

According to God's Word, He wants us to have an obedient heart. Proverbs 4:23-25, says "Keep thy heart with all diligence; for out of it are the issues of life." More personal ruin and eternal loss have been caused by a failure to protect the heart than all failures to protect material matters combined. Stubbornness or disobedience comes from the corrupt or foul talk; this should never be on the lips of one who truly trust the Lord. Each believer should focus his eyes on the wise path; concentrating on it and not being distracted; and his conduct should be upright or honorable, as he stays on level paths and does not turn aside to evil. We should remember; if God gives us a command, He will enable us to carry out the command, so we should not make excuses or blame others for our failures. Solomon warns us to stay on our guard and watch over our hearts because this is where life starts. We should not talk out both sides of our mouths; we are to avoid careless chitchat, white lies, and gossip. Solomon is basically stressing or emphasizing the importance of watching our heart by allowing our whole person to be controlled by God's Word. The heart is the "master-control" of life; a wrong heart always produces a wrong life. The heart should be guarded, for out of it comes one's actions. The word "Heart" means more than a mental or emotional capacity; it also includes

Live Life with a Heart Deeply Connected to God

one's values.

God does not want us to ignore our mind or common sense, He simply does not want us to lean only on them and reject His way. We are to keep our eyes straight ahead; ignore all sideshow distractions. If we watch our step, the road will stretch out smooth before us. Look neither to the right or left; leave evil in the dust. *Part of living a Christian life is focusing our hearts on spiritual matters.* God wants us to grow an obedient heart; a heart that receives His Word and a trusting heart that obeys His commandments.

Notes:

_____

_____

_____

_____

_____

_____

_____

_____

_____

_____

CHAPTER 7

POISON HEARTS TO GOOD NEWS

I ask that you honestly pray this prayer before reading this very important chapter, *"Poison Hearts to Good News."* Eternal God in Heaven, Creator of all things; I love and adore You. I give You thanks for Your grace and mercy. I give You thanks for Your Word. Now Lord, as Your Word penetrates my heart by Your Holy Spirit in reading this chapter, give me strength to be faithful and obedient to You and Your Word. Father God, allow Your Holy Spirit to open my heart with deep conviction and show me the importance of praying, studying, and meditating on Your Word. Help me Father God to make certain that I am a sincere obedient hearer and doer of Your Word. Lord, teach me how to live and serve You wholeheartedly according to Your will and Your plan for my life, and that I be a blessing to others. In Jesus' name I pray, Amen.

Luke 9: 3-5 (NKJV) reads as, "³ And He said to them, "Take nothing for the journey, neither staffs nor bag nor bread nor money; and do not have two tunics apiece.

⁴ "Whatever house you enter, stay there, and from there depart. ⁵ And whoever will not receive you, when you go out of that city, shake off the very dust from your feet as a testimony against them."

My beloved brothers and sisters in Christ Jesus, this is another opportunity to remember and celebrate the victorious work of our Lord and Saviour, Jesus Christ did on the cross. I am excited about this chapter because we have the liberty to become all that we can be in Jesus Christ. But this does not mean we have a license to do whatever we please. The worst bondage you can experience is living for yourself and yielding or giving way to the desires of the old nature. We have freedom to do good or evil, freedom to receive or reject Jesus Christ.

We must understand that Jesus Christ died that He might deliver us. We have the freedom to make the right choice! The gospel of the Lord should be a treasure to everyone. Everybody should want to experience the power of the Holy Spirit, and be an ambassador or witness for the Lord to the end of the earth. However, you will learn from this chapter that everybody is not a follower of the Lord and rejects God's Word and the messenger; I am the messenger today! As a preacher of the gospel (God's Word), I have learned through numerous letdowns and disappointments on this journey to the kingdom of God; people are just going to be people. Everyone is not going to listen, receive or obey God's Word or the messenger!

I realize that I will definitely not be treated better than our Lord and Saviour Jesus Christ. But I know that Jesus will never send me out to do a task without first giving me what I need. We are so prone to trust what we have, but we should trust in the Lord alone. If we are in God's will; He will supply our every need to do his will. Understanding God's Word has provided me peace and victory to become even stronger on overlooking God's rejecters of His Word; pray for the rejecters, and keep on moving. Some folks are determined to reject God's Word; no matter what.

There are many reasons why this is true, but they all boil down to one truth - - Satan (the devil). Satan has poisoned their hearts to the good news of God's Kingdom in Jesus Christ. Instead of beating our heads against a wall that the evil one has erected in the heart of some people, God calls us to keep moving on in our efforts to reach others. You see, we just don't have time for foolishness; we are to "shake their dust" off our feet and keep moving on!

Live Life with a Heart Deeply Connected to God

My charge since February 2005 is to: reach out to others, win souls for the Lord, lead people to Jesus Christ Jesus, be a witness for Jesus Christ, spread the gospel, preach the truth and nothing but the Truth and be a messenger of the gospel. If you are in the same family, Church, office, neighbourhood, or in the same home, and have regular closeness or proximity to people, and cannot move on; then we are called to live our faith before them and pray that our actions will demonstrate the faith; we profess and win them before the "Day of the Lord's" return.

The ruler of this world (the devil) has spiritually blinded the minds of many people who don't believe. They cannot see the light (the truth) of the Good News. The Good News about the glory of Jesus Christ. He is the One who is exactly like God (2 Corinthians 4: 4). In Biblical times, when leaving Gentile cities, pious Jews (pious is someone who is deeply religious and visibly or publicly follows all the moral and ethical codes of his religion).

When leaving Gentile cities; pious Jews often shook the dust from their feet to show their separation from Gentile practices. If the disciples "shook the dust" of a Jewish town from their feet, it would show their separation from Jews who rejected their Messiah. The gesture was to show the people that they were making a wrong choice. The opportunity to choose Christ might not present itself again!

According to the New Testament; when Jesus called His 12; He sent them into Jewish lands and told them, in a reversal, to perform the same act against the non-believing Jews (Matthew 10:14), and "it shall be more tolerable for the land of Sodom and Gomorrah in the day of judgment, than for that city" (Matthew 10:15). The only recorded instance of this practice in the New Testament was when Paul the Apostle and Barnabas were expelled from Antioch, Pisidia by Jews who disapproved of them teaching gentiles (Acts 13:50-51). Jesus called His twelve (12) apostles together; He gave them the power to heal sicknesses and power to force demons out of people. They had power and authority over all demons, and to cure diseases. Jesus sent the Apostles out to preach the kingdom of God and to heal the sick. He (He, meaning Jesus) - he said to the Apostles, Take nothing for the journey! "When you travel, don't take a Staff or walking stick!" Also, don't carry a bag, food, or money; take for your trip only the clothes you are wearing. Now, I would have probably responded to Jesus with all kinds of excuses when commanded to travel so light. Jesus said to His disciples, when you go into a house, stay there until it is time to leave. If the people in the town will not welcome you, go outside the town and shake their dust off of your feet. Shaking the dust from their feet" was used as testimony against those who were not listening or receiving God's preached Word -- This was a warning to them. So, the apostles went out; they traveled through all the towns. They told the Good News and healed people everywhere. Governor Herod heard about all these things that were happening. He was confused because some people said, "John the Baptizer has risen from death." Other people said, "Elijah has come to us." And some other people said, "One of the prophets from long ago has risen from death." Herod said, "I cut off John's head. So, who is this man I hear these things about?" Herod continued trying to see Jesus.

We cannot save or force people to change, but we can lead them to Jesus Christ. He can save and change them! When truth and love go together, and yet the message of God is rejected and despised, it leaves men without excuse and turns to a testimony against them. Governor Herod's guilty conscience was ready to conclude that John has risen from the dead. He desired to see Jesus and why did he not go and see Jesus?

Perhaps, because he thought; it was below or beneath him, or because he wished not to have any more reprovers or criticizers of sin. Delaying it, now Herod's heart was hardened, and when he did see Jesus, he was as much prejudiced against Jesus as others (Luke 23:11).

Even though some people will reject us and the invitation to Christ, keep sharing God's truth. When it comes to winning the lost, God wants His house filled, but when it comes to winning discipleship; Christ, thins out the ranks and wants only those who will die to self and live for Him. Receive the word of God with a sincere heart, and God will open your eyes and understanding of scriptures to tell others. Don't have a "Poison Heart to the Good News." If someone believes deeply in something, and lets everyone sees it through his or her behaviour, then he or she is pious; whether pious Christians or pious in something else; they are dutiful and obedient. Jesus is warning us to listen and receive His Word with a sincere heart. Think about what makes you serve the Lord; what makes you rejoice in the Lord; what makes you pause, and what makes you listen. Are you busy serving the lord or making self-important excuses? As servants of God, we have the privilege to tell the world - - come for all things are ready! Jesus has given us the commission, the power, and the message; there is no reason to be silent! We should have no problem giving the world a joyful witness. In God's world, for those who are sincere in seeking Him; there is no failure! But I must say; in an empty life without Jesus; is an opportunity for satan to move in and take over. But the devil is a liar, and the truth is not in him! Even the same people who give you joy today can also cause you sorrow tomorrow. Jesus Christ is for eternal life!

Notes:

_____

_____

_____

_____

_____

_____

_____

_____

_____

_____

_____

_____

_____

CHAPTER 8

MAINTAIN A JOYFUL HEART

As a child and adult, I was informed that happiness or laughter was good for the heart. I really did not take it to heart until later in my adult years. I believe I practiced joy and happiness in my life because of my mother's and others people's influence. But I did not fully understand until I was born again and became more acquainted with Proverbs 17:22, "A JOYFUL HEART IS GOOD MEDICINE, BUT A CRUSHED SPIRIT DRIES UP THE BONES." A JOYFUL HEART IS A GOOD MEDICINE! THIS SCRIPTURE AND FOLLOWERS OF JESUS ENABLED ME TO HAVE A joyful heart that dwells or stays on positive, peaceful thoughts. I did not feel joy or happiness when I allowed the negativity of others or awful situations to permeate my heart and mind. I felt so drained, unhappy and heated at times.

I chose happiness and laughter and instilled both in my children and grandchildren and others. Some people at times thought I was too happy but I refused to be restrained by someone else's negativity.

Live Life with a Heart Deeply Connected to God

I realize there are times when laughter is inappropriate or out of place; I will respect that but not be confined to foolishness or wickedness. I will maintain joy and happiness and surround myself with like-minded people who refresh or increase my joy and happy spirit. *Galatians 5:22 says, "But the fruit of the Spirit is love, joy, peace, patience, kindness, goodness, faithfulness."* The fruit of the spirit helped me feel joy even when I was struggling and going through some difficult and hard times with my guards down in my life. Some situations and experiences I encountered and went through were unquestionably challenging; I just wanted them to just go away. I found myself complaining about things that drained me emotionally and spiritually, not realizing how my joy was being stolen. The negativity I tolerated from others and some that I personally caused had to cease. When I decided to stop, think and learn how to overcome the negativity in my life caused by others and myself; I got closer and closer to God. I was able to praise Him like never before and have the joy I refused to let go or trade-in for worldly things or people. I feel so much better and can speak about praiseworthy things to God and others. Once you determine the root cause of being miserable or feeling joyless in life; it can help you avoid the onset of serious depression or unhappiness. I was truly hurting because I felt like the world was falling down on me; the concerns of my heart were overwhelming and virtually blinded my view to see many things that were taking place. I was in a painful season of anger and conflicts with others and guilt. I thank God for listening to my cries and healing my broken spirit with a joyful heart. *Proverbs 4:23, says "Above all else, guard your heart, for it is the wellspring (the fountain) of life." I made up my mind to have a joyful heart instead of a sad heart. If you are reading my book and have a sad heart, I want to encourage you to change and prepare your heart with joy and guidance from God's in Proverbs, Chapter 4.* If your heart is not devoted to God's purposes, it will lead astray and with a heart that's no pleasing to God. The Bible says a what's in a perverse heart will eventually come out in the life and the life is described as anything but beautiful or useful. That's why God's Word says in Proverbs 4:23, *"Above all else, guard your heart, for it is the wellspring (the fountain) of life."* God is telling us, above all else, guard your heart because everything we do, flows from our heart.

If you want to maintain a positive and joyful heart; avoid people with foolish behaviors. I've learned over several years the hard way; behaving foolishly and in the circle with foolish people keeps you in foolishness. Our behavior will become reckless without being aware of your recklessness. I realized and asked myself at times, what am I doing? What's wrong with you? This was a wake-up call for me but with consistent guidance and instructions from God. I realized some crazy things that I was doing that were not my character and conflicted within my heart. I constantly prayed to God for even a clearer picture of who I really am; this helped me to get my heart and life back on track. My heart returned back to joyfulness and peacefulness but not overnight. This was definitely a continuous process with the power of the Holy Spirt; praise God!!!

Notes:

_____

_____

_____

_____

_____

_____

_____

_____

CHAPTER 9

A LOVING HEART HAS NO PLACE FOR HATE

In Luke 6:43-45 (NLT), Jesus says, "a good tree can't produce bad fruit, and a bad tree can't produce good fruit. A tree is identified by its fruit. Figs are never gathered from thorn bushes and grapes are not picked from bramble bushes. A good person produces good things from the treasury of a good heart, and an evil person produces evil things from the treasury of an evil heart. What you say flows from what is in your heart.

A loving heart, has no place for hate; "Therefore, rid yourselves of all malice and all deceit, hypocrisy, envy, and slander of every kind. ²Like newborn babies, crave pure spiritual milk, so that by it you may grow up in your salvation (1 Peter 2:1-2). Just as a baby has an appetite for the mother's milk, so the child of God has an appetite for the father's (God's) word. If you lose that appetite and stop growing, check to see if any of the sins listed in 1 Peter 2:1 is infecting your life. I want to focus on hatred (malice): the dictionary defines Hatred as a "feeling." hatred can cause anger, or resentful emotional response, which can be used against certain people or ideas. But hatred is often

Live Life with a Heart Deeply Connected to God

associated with feelings of anger, disgust and a disposition or nature towards the source of hostility.

The former President of South Africa, Nelson Mandela said, "No one is born hating another person. People must learn to hate, and if they can learn to hate, they can be taught to love, for love comes more naturally to the human heart than its opposite." "Red, brown, yellow black and white - All are precious in His sight."
Everyone experiences hate and bitterness at some point in their life. Whether it's from friends, family, or coworkers; it happens to the best of us... As Christians or believers, we are called to live in ways that many simply won't understand... BECAUSE "The person without the Spirit does not accept the things that come from the Spirit of God but considers them foolishness, and cannot understand them because they are discerned only through the Spirit.

The New Living Translation: "But people who aren't spiritual can't receive these truths from God's Spirit (1 Corinthians 2:14). Jesus warned us that we would be hated. But he tells us to stand firm and do nothing. Luke 21:19, even goes as far as saying that we will win life. As hard as it may be, stand firm now to win later.

Live Life with a Heart Deeply Connected to God

1 Peter 2:1 shares that repentance was called for:
"Therefore, rid yourselves. Peter describes the ways in
which we fail to give love to each other. Peter listed five
sins of attitude and speech/actions which if harbored would
drive wedges between believers. Peter writes that we must
get rid of these five (5) attitudes and actions that oppose
love. In every case, they represent a choice to focus on my
benefit over and above the interests of someone else." The
five attitudes are malice, deceit, hypocrisy, envy and
slander. In a loving heart, these five attitudes have no
place, especially if one has been truly born again. If we
serve others before serving ourselves, this could put the
attitudes in their proper place, but not in a loving heart.

Jesus Christ can change an unloving heart that
possesses the five terrible attitudes that Peter describes in 1
Peter 2:1. Change that comes from the inside out makes
us like Jesus Christ: humble, bold, wise, holy, gracious,
encouraging, and faithful. Romans 12:1-2 reads,
"[1]Therefore, I urge you, brothers and sisters, in view of
God's mercy, to offer your bodies as a living sacrifice, holy
and pleasing to God this is your true and proper worship.

Live Life with a Heart Deeply Connected to God

[2]Do not conform to the pattern of this world, but be transformed by the renewing of your mind. Then you will be able to test and approve what God's will is- his good, pleasing and perfect will."

Change doesn't come easily, even if you understand God has your best interests in mind. However, the transformation of your heart and mind by Jesus will show your character and behavior properly aligned with the life of Christ. One must take the necessary steps to follow and obey God's voice; He will lovingly show you the way. Learning from wise counsel leads to wise behavior.

CHAPTER 10

THE HEART AND MIND MUST WORK TOGETHER

In the final chapter of my book, I want to re-emphasize the importance of living with a heart deeply connected to God and a lifestyle that is pleasing to God. In order to live a life pleasing to God and a heart deeply connected to God; one must have a humble and teachable spirit. In Matthew 22:37, [37]Jesus replied: "'Love the LORD your God with all your heart and with all your soul and with all your mind. The heart reveals the real you; it provides whether your heart is really deeply connected to God by your actions and behavior. Dr. Richards (2017), says "the heart is comprised of all our thoughts, feelings, beliefs and motives and it is the truest aspect of who we are. My heart is the real me." I totally agree with his suggestion and believe that our heart, when open to God will help us establish a deeply connected heart that God wants us to have a believer.

The heart and mind must be really important to be mentioned thousands of times throughout the Bible. The mind and heart are different but definitely needed to survive.

Live Life with a Heart Deeply Connected to God

Ephesians 2:8-10 (NKJV) records these words: "⁸ For by
grace you have been saved through faith, and that not of
yourselves; *it is* the gift of God, ⁹ not of works, lest anyone
should boast. ¹⁰ For we are His workmanship, created in
Christ Jesus for good works, which God prepared
beforehand that we should walk in them."

According to Ephesians 2:8-10, the heart and mind are
both necessary for biblical faith. We are saved through
faith; the mind and heart must both be engaged to have a
true personal relationship with God. You can passionately
worship a false version of God, and you can lifelessly
believe in a doctrinally accurate picture of God. God desires
us to love Him passionately and truly. The more we
passionately love God as a person, the more we will desire
to know the truth about him. And the more truth we learn
about Him from studying the Bible, the more we will
passionately love Him. The way we feel affects the way we
think, and the way we think affects the way we feel. We
are saved through faith (Ephesians 2:8-10). The mind and
heart must both be engaged in this process because to have
faith in God; we must believe and trust Him. Believing
requires the mind, but to trust someone requires the heart.

We are saved through believing certain facts about God. God sent His son into the world. Jesus died on the cross for our sins, God raised Jesus from the dead on the third day, Jesus ascended into heaven, and God sends His Spirit to dwell in people who become Christians. These are some of the most important facts we must believe to be Christians.

But if our faith ends with the beliefs of the mind, this is not saving faith. James 2:19 states, "You believe that there is one God. Good! Even the demons believe that—and shudder." In other words, satan believes the truth about God in his mind, but he does not live for God; he does not trust God. James 2 makes it very clear, faith without deeds is dead. This means that if we just believe certain facts, our faith is not genuine. Genuine faith affects the way we live. Our life will only be lived for God if we trust Him. So, to have saving faith, it requires belief and trust, which require the mind and the heart. Therefore, the mind and heart must both be changed through the power of the Holy Spirit (1 Corinthians 2:6-16, Ezekiel 36:26-27). Those who truly know God will love God with all of their heart and mind (Matthew 22:37).

Live Life with a Heart Deeply Connected to God

The heart and mind must work together in our personal relationship with God. When we engage our heart, an intimate relationship with God is established. The reasons why so many people do not have a personal relationship with God is because of his or her disbelief in God and practices of sin. When one has disbelief, no trust in God and practice sin; this hinders one's personal intimate relationship with God. I pray that what you read in this book will help you see the importance of opening your heart totally to God. Don't allow the things of the world and satan's corrupt craftiness to hinder or stop you from having a heart that's aligned with God's heart.

References

Richards, J. Dr. (2017). Daily Inspirations: What does it mean to connect to God's heart? Impact Ministries

Wolgemuth, Nancy, D. (2020). Holiness: The heart God purifies," *Article, Revive our Hearts,* https://www.reviveourhearts.com/articles/holiness-heart-god-purifies-discussion/

Made in the USA
Middletown, DE
28 October 2021